VISION 10

VISION 101

VISION FOR LIVING IN THE NEW MILLENNIUM

VISION 101

© 1999 Matthew Ashimolowo
Published by Mattyson Media an imprint of MAMM

Matthew Ashimolowo Media Ministries
57 Waterden Road
Hackney Wick
London
E15 2EE

All rights reserved. No part of this publication may be reproduced, stored in a retrieval system, or be transmitted, in any form, or by any means, mechanical, electronic, photocopying or otherwise without prior written consent of the publisher.

Bible quotes are from the King James Bible unless otherwise stated.
ISBN 1 874 646-25-2

VISION 101

WHAT IS VISION?

VISION 101

The unique fingerprint of God for your ministry, there is none like it.

"For I know the thoughts that I think toward you, saith the LORD, thoughts of peace, and not of evil, to give you an expected end."
Jeremiah 29:11

VISION 101

It is the picture you must have in the arena of your heart, of a preferred destination.

"But as it is written, Eye hath not seen, nor ear heard, neither have entered into the heart of man, the things which God hath prepared for them that love him." 1 Corinthians 2: 9

VISION 101

Focuses your life and pursuit.

"For the Lord GOD will help me; therefore shall I not be confounded: therefore have I set my face like a flint, and I know that I shall not be ashamed." Isaiah 50: 7

==================== **VISION 101** ====================

Vision empowers you to see and pursue a desired tomorrow.

"And Jabez was more honorable than his brethren: and his mother called his name Jabez, saying, Because I bare him with sorrow. And Jabez called on the God of Israel, saying, Oh that thou wouldest bless me indeed, and enlarge my coast, and that thine hand might be with me, and that thou wouldest keep me from evil, that it may not grieve me! And God granted him that which he requested." 1 Chronronicles 4: 9-10

VISION 101

Vision is like faith, it is the evidence in your heart of things hoped for.

"Now faith is the substance of things hoped for, the evidence of things not seen." Hebrew 11: 1

VISION 101

It is what you can use to inspire commitment.

"And the eyes of them that see shall not be dim, and the ears of them that hear shall hearken." Isaiah 32: 3

VISION 101

It helps you paint a mental portrait of your destination.

"To an inheritance incorruptible, and undefiled, and that fadeth not away, reserved in heaven for you." 1 Peter 1: 4

═══════ **VISION 101** ═══════

WHY YOU NEED VISION

VISION 101

It is a God imparted picture of your destiny and goal.

"And he laid it upon my mouth, and said, Lo, this hath touched thy lips; and thine iniquity is taken away, and thy sin purged. Also I heard the voice of the Lord, saying, Whom shall I send, and who will go for us? Then said I, Here am I; send me." Isaiah 6: 7,8

VISION 101

It is the key to authentic ministry.

"Whereupon, O king Agrippa, I was not disobedient unto the heavenly vision." Acts 26: 19

VISION 101

It helps you out of mediocrity, lock step ministry and copycat ministry.

"But we will not boast of things without our measure, but according to the measure of the rule which God hath distributed to us, a measure to reach even unto you." 2 Corinthians 10: 13

VISION 101

Vision is the glory of the end time church.

"And it shall come to pass afterward, that I will pour out my spirit upon all flesh; and your sons and your daughters shall prophesy, your old men shall dream dreams, your young men shall see visions."
Joel 2: 28

VISION 101

Vision gives you insight into Gods purpose for your life.

"And we know that all things work together for good to them that love God, to them who are the called according to his purpose."
Romans 8: 28

VISION 101

Visions from God come with peace.

"For the kingdom of God is not meat and drink; but righteousness, and peace, and joy in the Holy Ghost." Romans 14: 17

"Thou wilt keep him in perfect peace, whose mind is stayed on thee: because he trusteth in thee." Isaiah 26: 3

VISION 101

God given vision comes with a divine drive.

"For though I preach the gospel, I have nothing to glory of: for necessity is laid upon me; yea, woe is unto me, if I preach not the gospel!"
1 Corinthians 9:16

VISION 101

It is the doorway to a greater destiny.

"But as it is written, Eye hath not seen, nor ear heard, neither have entered into the heart of man, the things which God hath prepared for them that love him." 1 Corinthians 2: 9

VISION 101

Vision determines your destiny.

"For verily I say unto you, That whosoever shall say unto this mountain, Be thou removed, and be thou cast into the sea; and shall not doubt in his heart, but shall believe that those things which he saith shall come to pass; he shall have whatsoever he saith. Therefore I say unto you, What things soever ye desire, when ye pray, believe that ye receive them, and ye shall have them."
Mark 11: 23-24

VISION 101

Vision marks you for distinction.

"And Pharaoh said unto Joseph, Forasmuch as God hath shewed thee all this, there is none so discreet and wise as thou art: Thou shalt be over my house, and according unto thy word shall all my people be ruled: only in the throne will I be greater than thou."
Genesis 41: 39-40

VISION 101

Life finds meaning where there is vision.

"Behold, I will do a new thing; now it shall spring forth; shall ye not know it? I will even make a way in the wilderness, and rivers in the desert." Isaiah 43: 19

VISION 101

Vision turns potential to an active force.

"For ye see your calling, brethren, how that not many wise men after the flesh, not many mighty, not many noble, are called: ....; and God hath chosen the weak things of the world to confound the things which are mighty; And base things of the world, ... things which are not, to bring to nought things that are: That no flesh should glory in his presence." 1 Corinthians 1: 26-29

VISION 101

Vision is your key to worry free living.

"Not as though I had already attained, either were already perfect: but I follow after, if that I may apprehend that for which also I am apprehended of Christ Jesus. Brethren, I count not myself to have apprehended: but this one thing I do, forgetting those things which are behind, and reaching forth unto those things which are before, I press toward the mark for the prize of the high calling of God in Christ Jesus." Philippians 3: 12-14

VISION 101

The entrance of vision assures you that tomorrow will be alright.

"For I know the thoughts that I think toward you, saith the LORD, thoughts of peace, and not of evil, to give you an expected end."
Jeremiah 29:11

VISION 101

Great visions that are from God can pass on to your future generation.

"And he dreamed, ...And, behold, the LORD stood above it, and said, I am the LORD God of Abraham thy father,....the land whereon thou liest, to thee will I give it, and to thy seed; I am with thee, and will keep thee in all places whither thou goest, ..." Genesis 28: 12-15

VISION 101

Vision is the unique calling on your life which no one else is equipped to achieve.

"See, I have this day set thee over the nations and over the kingdoms, to root out, and to pull down, and to destroy, and to throw down, to build, and to plant." Jeremiah 1: 10-11

VISION 101

It is your eye into the future.

"While we look not at the things which are seen, but at the things which are not seen: for the things which are seen are temporal; but the things which are not seen are eternal." 2 Corinthians 4:18

VISION 101

God given visions creates strong desire or passion.

"(Not in your own strength) for it is God Who is all the while effectually at work in you (energising and creating in you the power and desire), both to will and to work for His good pleasure and satisfaction and delight." Philippians 2: 13 (Amplified)

VISION 101

God given visions are compulsive.

"For though I preach the gospel, I have nothing to glory of: for necessity is laid upon me; yea, woe is unto me, if I preach not the gospel!" 1 Corinthians 9:16

VISION 101

God given visions are life satisfying.

"Being confident of this very thing, that he which hath begun a good work in you will perform it until the day of Jesus Christ."
Philippians 1: 6

VISION 101

God given visions are revelatory in nature.

"For I neither received it of man, neither was I taught it, but by the revelation of Jesus Christ." Galatians 1: 12

VISION 101

God given visions bring a dividend not liability.

"Thus saith the LORD, thy Redeemer, the Holy One of Israel; I am the LORD thy God which teacheth thee to profit, which leadeth thee by the way that thou shouldest go." Isaiah 48: 17

VISION 101

God given visions are outlasting in scope.

"I know that, whatsoever God doeth, it shall be for ever: nothing can be put to it, nor any thing taken from it: and God doeth it, that men should fear before him." Ecclesiastes 3: 14

VISION 101

Your vision is the compass to lead you to your desired destiny.

"By faith Abraham, when he was called to go out into a place which he should after receive for an inheritance, obeyed; and he went out, not knowing whither he went." Hebrew 11: 8

"For he looked for a city which hath foundations, whose builder and maker is God." Hebrews 11: 10

VISION 101

Your vision helps you to focus your energy.

"For we are his workmanship, created in Christ Jesus unto good works, which God hath before ordained that we should walk in them."
Ephesians 2: 10

VISION 101

Vision gives the energy required for tough times.

"Looking unto Jesus the author and finisher of our faith; who for the joy that was set before him endured the cross, despising the shame, and is set down at the right hand of the throne of God."
Hebrews 12: 2

VISION 101

Vision increases your hope and faith level.

"Therefore it is of faith, that it might be by grace; to the end the promise might be sure to all the seed; not to that only which is of the law, but to that also which is of the faith of Abraham; who is the father of us all, ...Who against hope believed in hope, that he might become the father of many nations, according to that which was spoken, So shall thy seed be." Romans 4: 16b, 18

VISION 101

Vision seems to always inspire provision.

"And Abraham called the name of that place Jehovah jireh: as it is said to this day, In the mount of the LORD it shall be seen." Genesis 22: 14

"And Abraham said, My son, God will provide himself a lamb for a burnt offering: so they went both of them together." Genesis 22: 8

VISION 101

Only those who answer tomorrow's question today can see significant breakthrough.

"Thou shalt be over my house, and according unto thy word shall all my people be ruled: only in the throne will I be greater than thou."
Genesis 41: 40

VISION 101

The knowledge vision brings informs your decisions.

"And after he had seen the vision, immediately we endeavored to go into Macedonia, assuredly gathering that the Lord had called us for to preach the gospel unto them." Acts 16: 10

VISION 101

You are able to say no to what God has not led you to.

"For as many as are led by the Spirit of God, they are the sons of God."
Romans 8: 14

VISION 101

The knowledge vision brings is a key to productivity.

"If ye be willing and obedient, ye shall eat the good of the land."
Isaiah 1: 19

VISION 101

There is no future in anything, it is perceived and then created.

"We having the same spirit of faith, according as it is written, I believed, and therefore have I spoken; we also believe, and therefore speak." 2 Corinthians 4: 13

VISION 101

To be without vision is to be the most bankrupt person.

"Where there is no vision, the people perish: but he that keepeth the law, happy is he." Proverbs 29: 18

VISION 101

You are as small or as great as your vision.

"For as he thinketh in his heart, so is he: Eat and drink, saith he to thee; but his heart is not with thee." Proverbs 23: 7

VISION 101

Vision will speak of your destiny and not lie.

"For the vision is yet for an appointed time, but at the end it shall speak, and not lie: though it tarry, wait for it; because it will surely come, it will not tarry."   Habakkuk 2: 3

VISION 101

You can only make sense of the future by vision.

"Where there is no vision, the people perish: but he that keepeth the law, happy is he." Proverbs 29: 18

====== VISION 101 ======

Only visionaries grow in God's kingdom.

"And the child Samuel grew on, and was in favor both with the LORD, and also with men." 1 Samuel 2: 26

"Like newborn babies you should crave (thirst for, earnestly desire) the pure (unadulterated) spiritual milk, that by it you may be nutured and grow unto (completed) salvation." 1 Peter 2: 2 (Amplied)

VISION 101

Your future and function depends on it.

"I know that, whatsoever God doeth, it shall be for ever: nothing can be put to it, nor any thing taken from it: and God doeth it, that men should fear before him." Ecclesiastes 3: 14

VISION 101

The discovery of vision is the end of all struggles.

"For which cause we faint not; but though our outward man perish, yet the inward man is renewed day by day. For our light affliction, which is but for a moment, worketh for us a far more exceeding and eternal weight of glory; While we look not at the things which are seen, but at the things which are not seen: for the things which are seen are temporal; but the things which are not seen are eternal."
2 Corinthians 4: 16-18

VISION 101

Vision helps you to focus and not be a referee in other people's matter.

"Wherefore, brethren, look ye out among you seven men of honest report, full of the Holy Ghost and wisdom, whom we may appoint over this business. But we will give ourselves continually to prayer, and to the ministry of the word." Acts 6: 3-4

VISION 101

Vision is the medication that takes away stress.

"Better is an handful with quietness, than both the hands full with travail and vexation of spirit." Ecclesiastes 4: 6

VISION 101

Vision helps to locate your calling and begin to manifest it.

"And all Israel from Dan even to Beersheba knew that Samuel was established to be a prophet of the LORD." 1 Samuel 3: 20

VISION 101

Vision increases your speed in life.

"And the hand of the LORD was on Elijah; and he girded up his loins, and ran before Ahab to the entrance of Jezreel." 1 Kings 18: 46

VISION 101

Your future is in danger if you cannot see beyond your nose.

"The eyes of your understanding being enlightened; that ye may know what is the hope of his calling, and what the riches of the glory of his inheritance in the saints." Ephesians 1: 18

VISION 101

Vision makes your life unstoppable.

"Then Isaac sowed in that land, and received in the same year an hundredfold: and the LORD blessed him. And the man waxed great, and went forward, and grew until he became very great: For he had possession of flocks, and possession of herds, and great store of servants: and the Philistines envied him." Genesis 26: 12-14

VISION 101

Success follows diligent pursuit of vision.

"He that tilleth his land shall be satisfied with bread: but he that followeth vain persons is void of understanding." Proverbs 12: 11

VISION 101

There is no future in jobs or certificates it is in visionaries.

"I returned, and saw under the sun, that the race is not to the swift, nor the battle to the strong, neither yet bread to the wise, nor yet riches to men of understanding, nor yet favor to men of skill; but time and chance happeneth to them all." Ecclesiastes 9: 11

VISION 101

One person with vision outweighs 100 passive people.

"And Jabez was more honorable than his brethren: and his mother called his name Jabez, saying, Because I bare him with sorrow. And Jabez called on the God of Israel, saying, Oh that thou wouldest bless me indeed, and enlarge my coast, and that thine hand might be with me, and that thou wouldest keep me from evil, that it may not grieve me! And God granted him that which he requested." 1 Chronicles 4: 9-10

VISION 101

Visionaries make history others study it.

"And the LORD answered me, and said, Write the vision, and make it plain upon tables, that he may run that readeth it." Habakkuk 2: 2

VISION 101

If there is no vision, wastage is inevitable.

"Where there is no vision, the people perish: but he that keepeth the law, happy is he." Proverbs 29: 18

VISION 101

Your vision helps you to locate your place in the programme of God.

"For the which cause I also suffer these things: nevertheless I am not ashamed: for I know whom I have believed, and am persuaded that he is able to keep that which I have committed unto him against that day."
2 Timothy 1: 12

VISION 101

Your vision fires you up to solve certain problems.

"For if thou altogether holdest thy peace at this time, then shall there enlargement and deliverance arise to the Jews from another place; but thou and thy father's house shall be destroyed: and who knoweth whether thou art come to the kingdom for such a time as this?"
Esther 4: 14

═══ VISION 101 ═══

Your vision for life will be beyond your natural ability.

"I returned, and saw under the sun, that the race is not to the swift, nor the battle to the strong, neither yet bread to the wise, nor yet riches to men of understanding, nor yet favor to men of skill; but time and chance happeneth to them all." Ecclesiastes 9: 11

== VISION 101 ==

Vision focuses your life from panic and crises to success orientation.

"For thus saith the Lord GOD, the Holy One of Israel; In returning and rest shall ye be saved; in quietness and in confidence shall be your strength: and ye would not." Isaiah 30: 15

VISION 101

A visionary's life is at peace with itself.

"Not that I speak in respect of want: for I have learned, in whatsoever state I am, therewith to be content." Philippians 4: 11

VISION 101

Vision increases your confidence in God.

"Being confident of this very thing, that he which hath begun a good work in you will perform it until the day of Jesus Christ."
Philippians 1: 6

VISION 101

VISION TRUTHS

VISION 101

Vision helps you fulfil the law of sight.

"And the LORD said unto Abram, after that Lot was separated from him, Lift up now thine eyes, and look from the place where thou art northward, and southward, and eastward, and westward: For all the land which thou seest, to thee will I give it, and to thy seed for ever." Genesis 13: 14-15

VISION 101

Vision is not a product of consensus but works by it.

"And the things that thou hast heard of me among many witnesses, the same commit thou to faithful men, who shall be able to teach others also." 2 Timothy 2: 2

VISION 101

There is always need for a facilitator of vision to bring anything world-wide.

"Then the LORD put forth his hand, and touched my mouth. And the LORD said unto me, Behold, I have put my words in thy mouth. See, I have this day set thee over the nations and over the kingdoms, to root out, and to pull down, and to destroy, and to throw down, to build, and to plant." Jeremiah 1: 9-10

VISION 101

Aim for God's glory and true vision will be revealed.

"But as truly as I live, all the earth shall be filled with the glory of the LORD." Numbers 14: 21

==== VISION 101 ====

Vision needs to be articulated and made plain, so others can run with it.

"And the LORD answered me, and said, Write the vision, and make it plain upon tables, that he may run that readeth it."
Habakkuk 2:2

VISION 101

Visionaries cut out a path which others follow.

"Now all these things happened unto them for ensamples: and they are written for our admonition, upon whom the ends of the world are come."
1 Corinthians 10:11

VISION 101

Vision results in clear direction.

"And a vision appeared to Paul in the night; There stood a man of Macedonia, and prayed him, saying, Come over into Macedonia, and help us. And after he had seen the vision, immediately we endeavored to go into Macedonia, assuredly gathering that the Lord had called us for to preach the gospel unto them." Acts 16: 9-10

VISION 101

It is the way to move your life from Explanation to Exclamation.

"And Jabez was more honorable than his brethren: and his mother called his name Jabez, saying, Because I bare him with sorrow. And Jabez called on the God of Israel, saying, Oh that thou wouldest bless me indeed, and enlarge my coast, and that thine hand might be with me, and that thou wouldest keep me from evil, that it may not grieve me! And God granted him that which he requested." 1 Chronicles 4: 9-10

VISION 101

Vision helps you to innovate without waiting for problems.

"Through wisdom is an house builded; and by understanding it is established: And by knowledge shall the chambers be filled with all precious and pleasant riches." Proverbs 24: 3-4

VISION 101

Desire, enquire to acquire vision.

"Give therefore thy servant an understanding heart to judge thy people, that I may discern between good and bad: for who is able to judge this thy so great a people?" 1 Kings 3: 9

"One thing have I desired of the LORD, that will I seek after; that I may dwell in the house of the LORD all the days of my life, to behold the beauty of the LORD, and to enquire in his temple."
Psalm 27: 4

VISION 101

CRAVE - nothing is supplied by God if there is no craving for it.

"Blessed are they which do hunger and thirst after righteousness: for they shall be filled." Matthew 5: 6

VISION 101

You are responsible for finding following and finishing your vision.

"Wherefore seeing we also are compassed about with so great a cloud of witnesses, let us lay aside every weight, and the sin which doth so easily beset us, and let us run with patience the race that is set before us. Looking unto Jesus the author and finisher of our faith; who for the joy that was set before him endured the cross, despising the shame, and is set down at the right hand of the throne of God."
Hebrews 12: 1-2

VISION 101

Let your vision shape how you face life.

"Looking unto Jesus the author and finisher of our faith; who for the joy that was set before him endured the cross, despising the shame, and is set down at the right hand of the throne of God." Hebrews 12: 2

VISION 101

Find out God's plan that's where your future lies.

"Then shall we know, if we follow on to know the LORD: his going forth is prepared as the morning; and he shall come unto us as the rain, as the latter and former rain unto the earth." Hosea 6: 3

VISION 101

Walk with God you will reach your destination.

"Except the LORD build the house, they labor in vain that build it: except the LORD keep the city, the watchman waketh but in vain."
Psalm 127: 1

VISION 101

Write out your vision.

"And the LORD answered me, and said, Write the vision, and make it plain upon tables, that he may run that readeth it." Habakkuk 2: 2

VISION 101

Make the vision you see your confession.

"We having the same spirit of faith, according as it is written, I believed, and therefore have I spoken; we also believe, and therefore speak."
2 Corinthians 4:13

VISION 101

Work out your vision, nothing works until you act on it.

"Now he that planteth and he that watereth are one: and every man shall receive his own reward according to his own labor."
1 Corinthians 3: 8

VISION 101

Cultivate the habit of preparing well.

"Through wisdom is an house builded; and by understanding it is established: And by knowledge shall the chambers be filled with all precious and pleasant riches. A wise man is strong; yea, a man of knowledge increaseth strength." Proverbs 24: 3-5

VISION 101

Prayer is necessary to know God's mind.

"Then shall we know, if we follow on to know the LORD: his going forth is prepared as the morning; and he shall come unto us as the rain, as the latter and former rain unto the earth." Hosea 6:3

"As they ministered to the Lord, and fasted, the Holy Ghost said, Separate me Barnabas and Saul for the work whereunto I have called them." Acts 13:2

VISION 101

You will live a life, which is authentic and not synthetic.

"Now when they saw the boldness of Peter and John, and perceived that they were unlearned and ignorant men, they marvelled; and they took knowledge of them, that they had been with Jesus."
Acts 4: 13

VISION 101

Cultivate your levels of perception.

"And he saith unto them, Are ye so without understanding also? Do ye not perceive, that whatsoever thing from without entereth into the man, it cannot defile him." Mark 7:18

VISION 101

The greatest achievement of vision is what you make happen for others.

"And as ye would that men should do to you, do ye also to them likewise." Luke 6: 31

VISION 101

Develop and build your life around vision makers, mentors, healthy friends, loved ones, family.

"Be not deceived: evil communications corrupt good manners." 1 Corinthians 15: 33

VISION 101

Have no tolerance or excuse for dream takers.

"Ye have not yet resisted unto blood, striving against sin."
Hebrews 12: 4

VISION 101

Those who make exceptions and allow the negative are poisoning their vision.

"Then Jesus said unto them, Take heed and beware of the leaven of the Pharisees and of the Sadducees." Matthew 16: 6

VISION 101

Stay away from those who hate your dreams and make no investment in your life.

"And when they saw him afar off, even before he came ....And they said one to another, Behold, this dreamer cometh. Come now therefore, and let us slay him, and cast him into some pit, and we will say, Some evil beast hath devoured him: and we shall see what will become of his dreams." Genesis 37: 18-20

VISION 101

Put your life's goal in one clear, concise statement and commit yourself to it.

"And the LORD answered me, and said, Write the vision, and make it plain upon tables, that he may run that readeth it." Habakkuk 2: 2

VISION 101

Appoint mentors who should help you towards your intended goal.

"He that walketh with wise men shall be wise: but a companion of fools shall be destroyed." Proverbs 13: 20

VISION 101

Make up your mind and endeavour to break free from comfort zones.

"Now the LORD had said unto Abram, Get thee out of thy country, and from thy kindred, and from thy father's house, unto a land that I will shew thee: And I will make of thee a great nation, and I will bless thee, and make thy name great; and thou shalt be a blessing." Genesis 12:1

VISION 101

Get your vision straight, twisted vision makes you want to be someone else.

"For the Lord GOD will help me; therefore shall I not be confounded: therefore have I set my face like a flint, and I know that I shall not be ashamed." Isaiah 50: 7

VISION 101

It is a tragedy when visions are aborted, prematurely born, or result in being still born.

"And she said, The Philistines be upon thee, Samson. And he awoke out of his sleep, and said, I will go out as at other times before, and shake myself. And he wist not that the LORD was departed from him." Judges 16: 20

VISION 101

Dreams only come true for those who wake up.

"Wherefore he saith, Awake thou that sleepest, and arise from the dead, and Christ shall give thee light." Ephesians 5: 14

VISION 101

How you use the experience of life determines your distance in life.

"And not only so, but we glory in tribulations also: knowing that tribulation worketh patience; And patience, experience; and experience, hope: And hope maketh not ashamed; because the love of God is shed abroad in our hearts by the Holy Ghost which is given unto us." Romans 5: 3-5

VISION 101

The future responds to those who are ready to go all the way.

"If ye be willing and obedient, ye shall eat the good of the land."
Isaiah 1: 19

"But he that shall endure unto the end, the same shall be saved."
Matthew 24: 13

VISION 101

It does not take a lot of people in your life to bring out your destiny.

"Wherefore I put thee in remembrance that thou stir up the gift of God, which is in thee by the putting on of my hands." 2 Timothy 1: 6

VISION 101

Focus will make you move further ahead tomorrow than you are today.

"...turn not from it to the right hand or to the left, that thou mayest prosper withersoever thou goest." Joshua 1: 7b

VISION 101

The goals you set create new habits and atmospheres.

"Sow to yourselves in righteousness, reap in mercy; break up your fallow ground: for it is time to seek the LORD, till he come and rain righteousness upon you." Hosea 10: 12

VISION 101

If you do not do something about your vision all you will have is regrets.

"How long wilt thou sleep, O sluggard? when wilt thou arise out of thy sleep?" Proverbs 6: 9

VISION 101

Stop looking at where you are start looking at where you can be.

"While we look not at the things which are seen, but at the things which are not seen: for the things which are seen are temporal; but the things which are not seen are eternal." 2 Corinthians 4: 18

VISION 101

The abortion of potential condemns the future.

"For surely there is an end; and thine expectation shall not be cut off."
Proverbs 23: 18

VISION 101

God will not consult your past to determine your future.

"Remember ye not the former things, neither consider the things of old."
Isaiah 43: 18

VISION 101

Seeing the invisible helps you to do the impossible.

"Through faith we understand that the worlds were framed by the word of God, so that things which are seen were not made of things which do appear." Hebrews 11: 3

"By faith he forsook Egypt, not fearing the wrath of the king: for he endured, as seeing him who is invisible." Hebrews 11: 27

VISION 101

When you forget the pain of the past you will find the blessing of the future.

"Remember ye not the former things, neither consider the things of old. Behold, I will do a new thing; now it shall spring forth; shall ye not know it? I will even make a way in the wilderness, and rivers in the desert." Isaiah 43: 18-19

VISION 101

The vision you elevate, the ideal you talk about become what your life is built on.

"For by thy words thou shalt be justified, and by thy words thou shalt be condemned." Matthew 12: 37

VISION 101

Your vision shapes what you face in life.

"I will instruct thee and teach thee in the way which thou shalt go: I will guide thee with mine eye." Psalm 32: 8

"Looking unto Jesus the author and finisher of our faith; who for the joy that was set before him endured the cross, despising the shame, and is set down at the right hand of the throne of God." Hebrews 12:2

VISION 101

Success is the progressive achievement of the goals God helps you to set for your self.

"Though thy beginning was small, yet thy latter end should greatly increase." Job 8: 7

By little and little I will drive them out from before thee, until thou be increased, and inherit the land." Exodus 23: 30

VISION 101

Don't die in your winter, spring is coming.

"Thou therefore endure hardness, as a good soldier of Jesus Christ."
2 Timothy 2: 3

VISION 101

What you see in your spirit is what you get in material reality.

" While we look not at the things which are seen, but at the things which are not seen: for the things which are seen are temporal; but the things which are not seen are eternal." 2 Corinthians 4: 18

VISION 101

Life will send you all the ladders you need to climb; pain, problem, persecution, possibilities and opportunities.

"And we know that all things work together for good to them that love God, to them who are the called according to his purpose."
Romans 8: 28

VISION 101

Vision is the basis of living.

"Where there is no vision, the people perish: but he that keepeth the law, happy is he." Proverbs 29: 18

VISION 101

What you hear affects what you see, and what you see becomes what you get.

"So then faith cometh by hearing, and hearing by the word of God."
Romans 10: 17

VISION 101

Life treats you the way you treat yourself.

"For as he thinketh in his heart, so is he: eat and drink, saith he to thee; but his heart is not with thee". Proverbs 23: 7

VISION 101

Those who have not seen battles make boast of how strong they are.

"I returned, and saw under the sun, that the race is not to the swift, nor the battle to the strong, neither yet bread to the wise, nor yet riches to men of understanding, nor yet favor to men of skill; but time and chance happeneth to them all." Ecclesiastes 9: 11

VISION 101

When children are felling a tree the elders beholding can predict the direction of its fall.

"When I was a chld, I understood as a child, I thought as a child: but when I became a man, I put away childish things."
1 Corinthians 13: 11

VISION 101

The absence of foresight and planning made two brothers to die in slavery while trying to pay off six pence.

"Through wisdom is an house builded; and by understanding it is established: And by knowledge shall the chambers be filled with all precious and pleasant riches." Proverbs 24: 3-4